MW01292385

AGE OF ENLIGHTENMENT

A History from Beginning to End

Table of Contents

Introduction

The Age of Enlightenment is the defining intellectual and cultural movement of the modern world. In the simplest terms possible, the Enlightenment was born of the idea that all human beings share the same basic needs and as such should enjoy the same rights and privileges. Enlightenment philosophers believed that human reason, rationality, and benevolence would lead to the natural progression of society and the betterment of life on Earth. Intellectually, the Enlightenment gave birth to the disciplines of political science, economic theory, anthropology, sociology, and modern philosophy—disciplines which still form the basis of how we attempt to understand life in the twenty-first century. The Enlightenment can be understood as a direct challenge to the status quo at a time when intolerant and superstitious religious beliefs dominated most people's lives. Set free from the restraints of the Church, the state, and the monarchy, according to the Enlightenment, human beings would be able to improve society by focusing on developing the quality of material and social life.

Dating a movement is always a challenge and can never be strictly precise. Most historians agree that the Enlightenment began around the 1680s and lasted until the early 1800s. In Britain, the beginnings of enlightened thought can be traced back to the aftermath of the Glorious Revolution of 1688. Over a period of decades that began with the English Civil War, Britain was transformed from an autocracy led by the Stuart monarchy into a more constitutional society where religious tolerance was encouraged. In France, the death of Louis XIV in 1715 is often cited as the starting point of the Enlightenment, with the French Revolution of 1789 marking its end point. For some, the wellspring of enlightened thought can be found even further back in European history, around the 1620s when Europe experienced a surge of scientific inquiry, experimentation, and innovation.

For some historians, the Enlightenment was the direct result of the Renaissance and the Reformation. The Renaissance was the cultural rebirth of Europe. From its beginnings in fourteenth-century Italy, the Renaissance encouraged the revival of classical art, literature, and architecture and forced a massive shift from what we now refer to as medieval times to modern. The Renaissance prepared the western world for the Reformation that would shake the authority of the Church in Europe to its core.

Next came the Scientific Revolution, which would never have taken place had it not been for the philosophical groundwork of the Enlightenment. The final greatest cultural shift of the modern world that can be clearly linked to the Enlightenment was that of Modernity. While the scientific and industrial inventions, social advances, and revolutions in ways of thinking that defined the modern age cannot be traced directly back to the Enlightenment, it was the Enlightenment's core values that made this eventual shift possible.

The Enlightenment began as a philosophical group of ideas with the common themes of reason and progress. Before it was ever referred to as a movement, a project, or a historical phenomenon, the Enlightenment was simply an idea; the idea that a better understanding of our world and the people who occupy it could lead to the progression of our species and the betterment of the human condition on earth.

In this book we will look at this idea, how it evolved, diversified, and, eventually, changed the world.

Chapter One

The Great Thinkers of the Enlightenment

*"Sapere aude! 'Have courage to use your own reason!'-
that is the motto of enlightenment."*

—Immanuel Kant

There are some very significant differences between the beliefs of Enlightenment philosophers of different nations and different disciplines. Views held by certain French philosophers can differ dramatically from the beliefs of certain British economists, Spanish political thinkers, Irish novelists, etc. An incredibly diverse group, those thinkers and writers we now refer to as philosophers of the Enlightenment defy any easy classification. Above all else, the Enlightenment is best understood as a century of philosophy, and with this in mind, it is instructive to take a brief look at the Enlightenment's key thinkers, their lives, their writings, and their ideas.

The French – Montesquieu, Voltaire, Rousseau, Diderot, Condorcet

Paris has been a hub of intellectual, cultural and artistic movements for hundreds of years, and in the mid-eighteenth century, a particular group of Paris writers had a formative influence on the Enlightenment that gradually swept over Europe and beyond. Identifying themselves as "the philosophes," this group was inspired by writers such as Locke, Newton and Pierre Bayle. At the center of the philosophes was Montesquieu (1689-1755), a French man of letters who wrote the iconic *Spirit of the Laws* in 1748, a text often cited as representing the spirit of both the American and French revolutions. Trained as a lawyer, Montesquieu's theory of the separation of powers—into executive, legislative, and judicial, each of which are separate from each other and the power of the sovereign— was absolutely revolutionary at the time and paved the way for constitutions adopted by nations across the world, which are still in use today.

Another key philosopher was the ever-popular Voltaire (1694-1778) who used his literary skill to write plays, poems, novels, essays, and reams of letters that expressed his philosophical beliefs to the masses. Voltaire was extremely critical of the dogmatic nature of the Catholic Church and constantly campaigned for the separation of the French state and church. An advocate of freedom of expression and critic of all religious institutions, Voltaire's work was frequently censored, but in his writing, he often used satire to mask his true beliefs, as in his most famous work, *Candide*.

Another member of this group of enlightened Parisians was Rousseau (1712-1778), a philosopher, writer, and composer whose novel *Emilie, or On Education* was instrumental in educational reform in France. Rousseau's *Confessions,* published in 1789, is the first major published work of autobiography and helped to legitimize subjective writing as a valid art form. Rousseau was also a political theorist and was preoccupied with injustice and inequality in French society. His texts *Discourse on Inequality* and *The Social Contract* are considered some of the most influential works to come out of The Enlightenment.

Diderot (1713-1784) shared the mission of the other French philosophes and made an incredible contribution to the Enlightenment by co-founding, editing, and contributing to the *Encyclopédie*. The *Encyclopédie* was a 35-volume work, created between 1751 and 1772, with the aim of incorporating all of the world's knowledge into one text and, for many, represents the overall project of the Enlightenment.

Another Frenchman, the Marquis de Condorcet (1742-1794), used mathematics to inform his work in political science, creating the Condorcet method of calculating which candidate is most likely to win an election. Condorcet was passionate about the benefits of a liberal economy and constitutional monarchy and championed equal rights at a time when women and people of color were deemed second-class citizens in France.

All five of these French philosophes shared a common goal: to develop a society based on reason, natural law, and scientific endeavor, unencumbered by the oppressive doctrines of the Catholic Church. Almost all members of the aristocracy, the philosophes were not necessarily revolutionaries, nor did they all necessarily put class equality at the forefront of their agenda, but the ideas they promoted in their writings directly challenged the power of the monarchy and the Catholic Church in France, helping to pave the way for the world-changing French Revolution.

Descartes

Rene Descartes (1596-1650) was a contemporary of Francis Bacon and considered to be the father of modern western philosophy. Descartes' influence on the Enlightenment was profound. During his young adulthood, Descartes pursued a military career and lived in Holland, Italy, and France before accepting an invitation from Queen Christina of Sweden to write plays for her court. A mathematician and a physicist, Descartes believed that the material world was amenable to mathematical analysis and that the universe was ruled by a comprehensible cosmic order. Favoring Bacon's deductive method in his writings, Descartes' scientific works were considered dangerous enough to be banned by Louis XIV in France. Descartes argued for a dualistic understanding of existence, that human beings are composed of both matter and spirit, and coined the famous phrase, "I think, therefore I am."

Rene Descartes' work challenged the religious dogma of the time, yet the man himself was religious and believed in the existence of God. Like Descartes, other Enlightenment philosophers such as Isaac Newton, Christian Wolff, and John Locke took a moderate approach to religion and attempted to straddle the line between traditional systems of faith and new enlightened philosophies. Seeking to encourage a reform of the traditional ways of thinking and way of life in Europe, these philosophers were challenged by those who sought to destroy the status quo completely.

The English - Francis Bacon, Thomas Hobbes, and John Locke

Francis Bacon (1561-1626) was a member of the English aristocracy, a philosopher, a writer, a statesman, and a scientist. Bacon died before the Enlightenment really took hold across Europe, but his work in the field of science influenced many of the Enlightenment's key philosophers. Most notably, Bacon developed the inductive method of scientific inquiry. This approach, which seems like common sense today, stressed that observation and reason are the two components needed to come to a conclusion. Known as the father of empiricism, Bacon introduced the concept of scientific method during a time when faith-based solutions were offered for practical problems.

Thomas Hobbes (1588-1679) was a philosopher and political theorist whose text published in 1651, *Leviathan*, is credited with jolting the English Enlightenment into being. While Hobbes believed in an absolute monarchy, he was also a liberal and wrote on the rights of the individual, social equality, and the necessity of a political system that is based on the consent of its nation's people. Hobbes' controversial *Leviathan* posited that all human beings are inherently self-driven and that political communities must be built on a "social contract," ideas that inform political philosophy to this day.

John Locke (1632-1704) began his career as an Oxford academic, but in 1667, Locke became personal secretary and physician to the Earl of Shaftesbury and grew deeply involved in politics. Together Shaftesbury and Locke sought to decrease the power of the monarchy in Britain and restore the Catholic Church as the main religion. Locke was a supporter of the Glorious Revolution of 1688 and became a major beneficiary of its success. Locke's writings are preoccupied with attempts to find a middle-way between understandings of traditional religion and modern science. His most famous publication is *An Essay Concerning Human Understanding* (1690), in which he stated that knowledge was acquired through sensory and not divine means, and that only certain things could be known to be fact, laying the foundation for intellectual humility.

The Scots – Francis Hutcheson, Adam Smith, and John Hume

Francis Hutcheson (1694-1746) was a key member of the early Scottish Enlightenment. Born in Ireland, Hutcheson studied and lived in Glasgow before returning to his native land where he opened a private school. After writing a series of well-received essays on ethics and aesthetics, Hutcheson was invited to fill the coveted role of Chair of Moral Philosophy at the University of Glasgow. Hutcheson's main contribution to the Enlightenment was his writings on moral sense, a follow-up to Shaftesbury's earlier doctrine. Hutcheson famously said that virtue could be defined as "the greatest happiness of the greatest number."

A student of Hutcheson, Adam Smith (1723-1790) was the founder of liberal economic theory. Another key name in the Scottish Enlightenment, Smith grew up in a respectable family just north of Edinburgh and studied at Oxford, as Hutcheson had done, before taking on a teaching position at the University of Glasgow. Traveling in Europe as tutor to the Duke of Buccleuch, Smith met Voltaire and other leading philosophes who greatly inspired his later writings. In 1776, Smith published *Wealth of Nations*, the text that founded modern economic liberalism. Smith's work recognized the force of self-interest in economics while calling for a moral sense that was informed by sympathy and beneficence, a revolutionary idea at the time.

Another Scottish philosopher, David Hume (1711-1776), contributed to the Enlightenment in ways which led to a lasting impact on Western philosophy as a whole. Born into the Edinburgh gentry, Hume worked in a number of different jobs throughout his life including tutor, clerk for a sugar company, librarian, and secretary. In 1766, Hume offered Jean-Jacque Rousseau refuge in England and supported his extensive writings, but eventually, the pair fell out. Hume wrote *The History of England*, published in six volumes between 1754 and 1762 to public acclaim, and his main philosophical contribution to the Enlightenment was *A Treatise of Human Nature: Being an Attempt to Introduce the Experimental Method of Reasoning into Moral Subjects*.

The Germans – Leibniz, Wolff, and Kant

Gottfried Wilhelm Leibniz (1646-1716) is considered one of the most brilliant minds of the Enlightenment and is known as the founder of the Aufklärung or German Enlightenment. Leibniz began his career as a legal administrator in Leipzig and spent time as a courtier in the various courts of Hanoverian princes and the court of St Petersburg. A strange blend of scientist and spiritualist, Leibniz is credited with the discovery of calculus but couldn't support philosophy that relied solely on empirical evidence. Instead, Leibniz developed a theory of the universe that included a spiritual component, insisting on the existence of God and his creation of the world using metaphysical building blocks he called monads.

Greatly inspired by the work of Leibniz, Christian Wolff (1679-1754), studied and gained his master's degree in northern Germany. Wolff worked for a time at the University of Halle teaching mathematics and natural sciences, but his teachings, and his insistence that reason alone could form the basis of ethics was unpopular amongst orthodox philosophers of the time. Wolff was sent into exile by King William I of Prussia only to be invited back to Germany as a distinguished philosophy professor by his next in line, King Frederick II. Wolff published a huge number of works, 29 volumes in German and 41 in Latin, and made a significant contribution to the Enlightenment in his logical approach to encyclopaedism.

Immanuel Kant (1724-1804) remains one of the most well-known western philosophers of all time. Known as a skeptic philosopher, Kant built on David Hume's theories, attempting to reconcile rationalism and religious belief. Kant lived his whole life in Prussia and following his university education taught mathematics and natural sciences. Kant effectively restored the transcendental element of philosophical thought and is considered by some to have helped bring about the end of the Enlightenment. His key text, *Critique of Pure Reason* (1781), directly challenged other enlightenment philosophers and argued that all human beings are born with innate experiences that inform their perspective on the world. Kant theorized that nothing can be known, only perceived through the senses and perspective of the individual, and as such pure reason is an invalid approach to thought.

Chapter Two

Engaging With Religion

"Education is the kindling of a flame, not the filling of a vessel."

—Socrates

As a philosophical movement, the Enlightenment was composed of a chorus of disparate voices. As demonstrated in the previous chapter, Enlightenment thinkers differed in their perspective on a number of issues as often as they agreed. With that said, the Enlightenment is regarded as having been being profoundly anti-religious. Some Enlightenment philosophers were openly against religion in all its forms. Revolutionary atheists, these philosophers saw all religion as delusion and encouraged an understanding of the world that was rational and scientific. Other Enlightenment philosophers felt that there was still a place for religion in society, but that religious observance should be an optional extra and not a mandatory component of life.

Those who held a more moderate attitude towards religion tended to be united in their dislike of the Roman Catholic Church, an institution that used to hold unimaginable power and wealth and, some might argue, still does. There were also those Enlightenment philosophers who remained committed to their religion even as they deconstructed its history and role in society. For these philosophers, Enlightenment thought was religious in origin, as it stemmed from an intellectual curiosity of their own faith. The attitude towards religion during the Age of Enlightenment ranges from radical atheism to intellectually-curious faith and everything in between.

The Law of Nature or Natural Law

In order to understand the different ways the Enlightenment engaged with religion, we must first understand the history and role of religion in sixteenth-century Europe.

Before the Enlightenment movement took hold, the majority of academics were theologians. The study of God was at the center of intellectual inquiry; theology was considered the mother of sciences. Throughout the Middle Ages, and even into the eighteenth century in some parts of Europe, all study of morals, psychology, law, justice, and epistemology were carried out as an extension of the study of God.

Christians agreed that Christianity was a revealed religion. Christ had sacrificed himself for mankind in order to secure their salvation, and this knowledge was revealed to the masses through the medium of The Bible, the literal Word of God. The trouble was that Christians also agreed to the law of nature, a code of behavior defined by God that applied to all human beings, regardless of whether they were Christians or not. This natural law was a duty that all human beings owed to the God that had created them, although obedience to natural law would not bring about their salvation—only belief in the revelation could secure that. These two spheres, the study of God and his revelation and the study of natural, or human, sciences, had up until the seventeenth century been completely intertwined.

Referring only to the words of the Christian God via the Bible, academics found few answers to the larger questions they had about the nature of man and existence, so they turned to the work of the Ancient Greeks. Painstakingly reading, re-reading, and analyzing a small number of key texts, these theologian scholars borrowed so much from the work of Aristotle he became known simply as The Philosopher.

As we moved into the seventeenth century, natural scientists and philosophers began to criticize this approach to theology and sought to forge a separation between the study of God and the natural and human sciences. The idea that natural and human sciences could only be understood on the basis of direct experience gained authority and revolutionized the intellectual landscape of the Western world. By challenging the theologian's singular approach to knowledge, the door suddenly swung open to all kinds of scientific and philosophical exploration.

It was around this time that Galileo famously challenged the Church's doctrine that the Sun revolved the Earth, presenting his scientific findings that showed the opposite. Too far ahead of his time, Galileo was forced to refute his claim to avoid being burned at the stake as a heretic, and yet his discovery was correct—he later became the most celebrated champion of this new science.

Wars of Religion and Reformation

This astonishing transformation in the Western world's approach to religion was made possible by two major historical events, the devastating Wars of Religion and the Reformation that started them.

In the sixteenth century, Martin Luther and John Calvin had succeeded in bringing about a major religious reform in Europe. These theologians were the first to tackle some of the dogmas of the ancient faith of Christianity and subject them to individual reason. Their revolt against the Church and the split it caused in society was one of the leading causes of the numerous Wars of Religion that raged across Europe between the mid-sixteenth and mid-seventeenth centuries.

The French Wars of Religion (between 1562 and 1598), The English Civil War (1642-1651), and the Eighty Years War between Spain and the Netherlands (1568-1648) divided Europe along the lines of faith and turned the whole continent into an on-off killing field. The Thirty Years War (1618-1648) that enveloped the majority of central and eastern Europe, and killed millions, was the most devastating of these conflicts. Desperate to avoid a repeat of this barbarous war, theologians tried to initiate religious reform; meanwhile, Enlightenment scholars wanted to remove the power of organized religion altogether.

Theologians sought to avoid conflict by restoring faith to its very roots, advocating a study of the Word of God alone in the optimistic hope that everyone would agree on its literal interpretation. John Locke carried out what he deemed to be an "unprejudiced examination" of the Bible and first promoted the idea of separation of church and state. Locke argued that the state had no authority when it came to individual conscience and that a rational society must be responsible for their own moral code. These ideas were instrumental in the development of the American colonies and instructed Thomas Jefferson in drafting the United States Constitution. Jefferson called for a "wall of separation between church and state" and penned the "Jefferson Bible," a text that put the moral code of the New Testament at its forefront and gave no mention of miraculous events or Jesus Christ's resurrection.

Some Enlightenment thinkers from both moderate Protestant and Catholic backgrounds looked to the monarchy to enforce tolerance. Far from being a one-and-for-all stand on religion that promoted diversity and free speech, tolerance was simply an acknowledgment that the only way to create civil peace was to sanction opposing religious beliefs while keeping them far enough away from each other to avoid conflict. In 1651, political philosopher Thomas Hobbes published *Leviathan* in which he argued that the clergy was the greatest threat to civil peace and that in order to maintain a peaceful society a sovereign must demonstrate absolute power over public expression. Spinoza wrote on a similar theme in his *Theologico-Political Treatise* (1670), in which he argued that the freedom to philosophize posed no danger to the state.

Voltaire's *Traité sur la Tolérance* (1763) became the key text in the Enlightenment case for tolerance. In it, he deconstructed the current French society and argued that ancient civilizations had been more tolerant of each other than French citizens presently were. Voltaire argued that tolerance was essentially a matter of manners and that civilized society could only flourish if its members were respectful of each other's differences.

Enlightenment Histories of Religion

Other Enlightenment scholars looked to diminish the power of organized religion by examining it from a historical perspective. By looking back at the early church, Ancient Greek and Roman history, and more recent Christian doctrines, it became apparent that there were many ways to understand the meaning of grace and salvation. The authority of Christian teachings and The Bible itself came under scrutiny. Theorists posited that there is no such thing as the Word of God, as there was no original text, and what text there was had already been subject to a number of interpretations. The implications of this historical investigation into faith were far-reaching and inspired many Enlightenment thinkers to consider an entirely new approach to religion.

Importantly, Spinoza argued that the Bible should be read as the historical narrative of the ancient Hebrews. While the Bible offered a blueprint for effective social living, promoting piety, love for one's neighbor, and justice, it did not contain the Word of God and was better understood as a document of sacred history for Jews and Christians.

A more radical approach to religion was adopted by a group of thinkers who later became known as Deists. Headed by Irish intellectual John Toland, the Deists were a group of freethinkers who believed in the existence of a God, but not necessarily Christ. Arguing against the "mystery" of Christianity, Toland insisted that scripture could be understood by anyone with reason and the ability to read it. Other thinkers proposed atheism, such as Pierre Bayle, who hypothesized that atheists could still be moral, social creatures, but most Enlightenment thinkers were critics of Orthodox faiths, not religious faith itself. John Locke's famous *Letter Concerning Toleration* also tackled religious tolerance but argued from an overtly Protestant stance that all Christian men and women were responsible for themselves and each other in the eyes of God, a swipe at the Catholic faith that relied on the Church to communicate with God on the individual's behalf.

Many Enlightenment thinkers approached religion from a position that was less radical than atheism or deism, but that proved to be incredibly subversive in the long run. In 1757, David Hume published his *Natural History of Religion*. Rejecting the trend towards historical narrative, Hume put forward his theory that polytheism (belief in more than one God) or idolatry was the first religion of man and criticized Christianity as being the worst form of monotheism (the belief that there is only one God) because of its focus on salvation in the next world to the detriment of what is considered moral and just in this world.

Voltaire's essay *Universal History* (1722) directly tackled the notion that Christian and Jewish religious histories were the only sacred subjects worthy of study. Voltaire began his study of world history in China and traced his way west, demonstrating that Christianity and Judaism are the offspring of Islam.

For other writers such as d'Holbach, who published his late friend Boulanger's laboriously titled work *Antiquity unveiled by its Practises, or a Critical Examination of the Principal Religions and Political Opinions, Ceremonies and Institutions of the different Peoples of the Earth* (1766), recognized that history supplied the framework for understanding religion and that to study religious practices was to study the history of man in society. The most illuminating of the many histories of religion penned during the Enlightenment was the *Decline and Fall of the Roman Empire* (1776-88) by Edward Gibbon. Incredibly controversial on its release, *Decline and Fall* engaged with the beliefs of both Christians and Muslims and attempted to chart the history of both the Church and the Empire, faith and society, and the civil and the sacred side by side. Far from attacking religion as nonsensical or arguing for a radical removal of the powers of the Church, these Enlightenment thinkers contributed to secularization by a careful, considered process of historical inquiry, looking not to the Gods for answers but to fellow men, here on earth.

Chapter Three

Morality in the Age of Enlightenment

"Enlightenment means taking full responsibility for your life."

—William Blake

Before the eighteenth century, moral philosophy in Europe could only be understood through the lens of "natural law." Natural law is essentially a code of behavior passed down from God and applicable to all humans, which upholds the natural order of things. According to a pre-eighteenth-century view of natural law, certain values and rights are an inherent part of human nature that can be understood by everyone through the application of reason. Some Enlightenment philosophers argued that people were designed to act rationally, without the hand of God, and if allowed to exercise their reason without the restraints of the state or church, they could be relied upon to act in a way that would further the happiness of others.

This utopian ideal of natural law argued that human progress and betterment was possible through education and the improvement of the individuals' material and social life. The free man's natural pursuit of self-interest would benefit society while the free man's inherent sense of reason would guarantee sound moral judgments. Put another way; it is only through man's freedom that the true natural law can operate.

Natural law and how it worked in society was at the very heart of Enlightenment thought. The idea that the betterment of the human condition was inevitable provoked a diverse but passionate array of responses.

Followers of different religions adjusted the concept of natural law to suit their particular beliefs, giving emphasis to some values while diminishing the importance of others. Protestant philosophers tended to promote the idea that doing good for others mattered above all else, while Catholics stressed the importance of personal piety, insisting that individuals needed the guidance of the Church on specific moral issues.

Hobbes' *De Cive* (1642) directly challenged the Protestant ideal, insisting that man could only be a sociable creature when forced to be so by a sovereign power. For Hobbes, man's natural state was one of uncontrollable passions, utterly unsuited to sociable living, and an autocratic leader was needed to keep civilization in check. A number of thinkers responded to Hobbes' description of man's natural state as a "reign of passions" by looking at sociability as something that was solved over time.

German philosopher Samuel Pufendorf suggested that man was not innately sociable but had become so over time. Way before the institution of the state, men and women had come together and had begun to live under the shared values of the law of nature thanks to reason and reason alone. John Locke offered a theory somewhere between these two positions in his *Two Treatises on Government*. Locke famously stated that "in the beginning, all the world was America," referring to the continent that had only recently been discovered, and traced how society in Europe had been transformed through the introduction of property, the invention of money, and the subsequent desire for wealth.

Moral philosophy and the issue of natural law in modern society preoccupied a succession of English, Irish, and Scottish philosophers in the mid-eighteenth century. For Frances Hutcheson, our sense of morality could be understood, like taste, to have derived from a natural sentiment of kindness towards others. Pulling away from the strict Scottish Presbyterian position, Hutcheson did not acknowledge that the Christian promise of a rewarding afterlife was enough to keep morality in check, but he did point to God as instilling this natural morality in all of his subjects.

David Hume took this idea further but controversially cut God out of his theory altogether. Hume agreed that all human beings possess an innate benevolence, but that benevolence was only put into action "as a result of a process of sympathy" and that the virtue of justice was far from natural and only sanctioned over time. With no acknowledgment of God or natural law, Hume argued that morality and sociability are historical constructs that have been developed over time to serve a specific purpose.

Adam Smith took on the concept of sympathy and made it the foundation of his exploration of the betterment of the human condition in his *Theory of Moral Sentiments* (1759). According to Smith, moral judgments were made as the result of sentiments, not reason. In a society that was already experiencing extreme inequality, Smith saw that people were sympathetic with those who bettered themselves at the expense of others because they sought to emulate them. The foundation of our morals came from our need to see ourselves through the eyes of others.

It is at this point that Immanuel Kant took center stage and ushered in a new philosophic idealism that returned to natural law. Teaching as a professor of philosophy at Konigsberg University in Germany, Kant sought to shift Enlightenment philosophy, which was edging into ever more skeptical territory, back to an understanding of morals as the result of reason. Kant argued that individual moral autonomy provided the basis for the public application of reason and insisted that this idea alone defined Enlightenment.

According to Kant, the senses played a vital role in acquiring knowledge, but that knowledge must then be interpreted by the mind's unique internal patterns. These patterns are a part of our individuality and are in existence before we have any sensory experience. Some truths, Kant insisted, could not be found through scientific study or any engagement with the material world. Morals, religion, truth, beauty; these things existed beyond the material world and could not be proven to exist, but were known to human beings through pure reason. Pure reason was, for Kant, the highest form of human endeavor, built into human nature. Reason alone was a valid source of moral judgment and religious belief.

Kant's *Critique of Pure Reason* (1781) contained the majority of his ideas, while his later essays *Groundwork of the Metaphysics of Morals* (1785) and *Idea for a Universal History with a Cosmopolitan Purpose* (1784) focused on his idea of the "categorical imperative." If, Kant argued, we are to become a truly moral society we must accept the standard of the categorical imperative: "act in accordance with a maxim that can at the same time make itself a universal law." Kant acknowledged that the prevalence of passions in man, outlined by Hobbes, meant that rivalry and conflict were unavoidable, and those who abided by the rule of categorical imperative were never going to win the race towards material betterment.

Chapter Four

Society in the Age of Enlightenment

"The source of every crime, is some defect of the understanding; or some error in reasoning; or some sudden force of the passions."

—Thomas Hobbes

The Enlightenment philosophers who tackled historical narrative did so in a way that had never been seen before. Rather than looking at political events as isolated incidents, Enlightenment historians took into account the social and economic framework within which they took place. These writers took into account the different social structures, economic circumstances, and geographic locations of different nations and considered how the beliefs and traditions of their people might impact historical narrative. This seems like an obvious way to approach historical analysis now, but at the time this perspective was revolutionary. For the first time history was conceived of as "progress."

Going right back to what they believed was the beginning, some historians began to study animals. The English naturalist Edward Tyson conducted an influential study in 1699 where he represented a young orangutan as capable of walking on two legs and being in possession of vocal organs capable of speech. The line between human and animal was shown for the very first time to be somewhat blurred.

Other Enlightenment historians focused on humanity, exploring why some human societies had developed in certain ways while others hadn't. Adam Smith's *Wealth of Nations* offers the most influential theory of social progress, classifying progress into four stages: hunting, pastoral, agricultural, and commercial. Smith argued that society progressed from one mode of living to another through the "natural progress of opulence," or the quest for material wealth.

Language was also explored as a means of progress. It had previously been believed that language was merely one of God's gifts to man, but some historians looked at language acquisition and development as a key component of the evolution of our species. The general consensus of the time was that language played a key role in civilizing a nation and defining the spirit of its law of nature, or "manners." In theory, the more civilized a society, the more sophisticated its language would be and the more refined its morals and behavior.

One measure of how sophisticated and refined a society had become was how respectfully it treated its women. Women were previously considered unworthy of being the subject of historical narrative, but around the late eighteenth century women's histories began to be published, such as *The History of Women from the Earliest Antiquity* (1779), and a handful of women were acknowledge as writers of history themselves, such as

Catherine Macaulay who wrote the epic *History of England* (1763-83).

The progress of society was at the forefront of the work of a group that later became known as religious humanitarians. There was a clear correlation between the Enlightenment's concern for individual human worth and the betterment of the human species and traditional Christian principles that promoted community and goodwill towards others. Rather than theorizing the history of progress and hypothesizing on where it would go in the future, religious humanitarians sought to actively relieve human suffering amongst the urban poor, slaves, prisoners, and children. Religious humanitarians pushed for legal and prison reform and were inspired by rational Enlightenment thinkers' focus on education to bring Sunday Schools to England.

A specific outcome of this movement was the abolition of slavery in England. In 1774, slavery was made illegal in England, and for subsequent decades, a dedicated movement led by William Wilberforce (1759-1833) campaigned for the end of the slave trade worldwide. The efforts of Wilberforce and his supporters, including Evangelical Christians, Methodists, and Quakers, were rewarded in 1807 when the slave trade was ended, but it took another three decades before slavery was abolished in the British colonies.

Anti-imperialism was also aligned with Enlightenment thought. European engagement with people of colonized or simply exotic lands was routinely criticized by Enlightenment thinkers. Diderot's *The History of the Two Indies* (1770-1780) was highly critical of the behavior of

Europeans within the colonies, their treatment of native peoples, and their ownership of slaves. Adam Smith and Kant also offered rigorous critiques of aggressive strategies and monopolistic trading in the colonial world.

Amongst all of the positive enforcement of the idea of social progress and human betterment, and negative commentary on the evils of the Empire, one Enlightenment philosopher stood out. Rousseau refused to accept the view that history can be read as a progressive improvement of society and focused on inequality and man's ambiguous morals to emphasize how little progress had actually been made. Rousseau named the institution of property as the main cause of inequality in modern society. Language had only developed, he argued, when men and women began to live together in communities and had to negotiate the world of property and ownership of land. In verbally accepting the institution of ownership of land and property, we agreed to hierarchy and thus inequality.

In Rousseau's history of Europe, the central motivating force was not progress but corruption. According to Rousseau, the savage man "breathes nothing but repose and freedom" and "lives within himself," while the modern civilized man "sweats, scurries, constantly agonises" and "is capable of living only in the opinion of others."

Chapter Five

Science and Political Economy in the Age of Enlightenment

"Man is an animal that makes bargains: no other animal does this—no dog exchanges bones with another."

—Adam Smith

While the leading figures of the Enlightenment were considered philosophers rather than scientists, many of these figures had backgrounds in science. Scientific advancement is only possible through empirical processes and rational thought, and as such became strongly associated with the reason-based philosophies of Enlightenment thinkers. Initiated by early theological scholars who became dissatisfied with their attempts to understand life on earth through the prism of religious doctrine, scientists sought to understand the world in a material sense, using scientific methods to root knowledge in that which could be rationally proven. For Enlightenment philosophers, the overthrow of traditional institutions such as the Church and monarchy became a necessary step in the development of truly free thought and the continuation of scientific progress.

Although unmatched by the scientific revolution that followed it, the Enlightenment did lead to a number of important scientific discoveries and inventions. Most notably, chemist Joseph Black discovered carbon dioxide, geologist James Hutton proposed the existence of deep time, and James Watt invented the steam engine. Science was divided up into the study of physics, chemistry, natural history, biology, geology, mineralogy, and zoology. Astronomical discoveries influenced the way individuals saw themselves in the context of the universe, and Newton's law of gravity contributed to the idea that human reason could only operate effectively through the interpretation of sensory experience. Material reality became the only reality.

Adam Smith's *Wealth of Nations* represented a landmark in economics and placed political economy at the heart of Enlightenment thought. For Smith and his fellow Scot, Hume, commerce held the key to Europe's economic development and could be relied upon to benefit society at every level. Smith insisted that the wealth of a nation must be measured by its per capita income; to be a truly commercial, modern society, that figure must constantly increase. These Scottish economists directly challenged Rousseau's contention that society must grow in a balanced way, with growth split equally between city and countryside. For Smith, only a commercial society, in which every individual acted in their own self-interest but was driven by competition, would improve everybody's life for the better. Government regulation had a negative impact on this growth, so individuals should be left to their own initiative to drive market forces.

Outside of the university, Smith's assertions were being put to the test in the real world. In the early to mid-eighteenth century, the rise of commercialism and manufacturing produced a rapidly growing population in the major civilian centers of the West. Thanks to agricultural reform, particularly in England, better food supplies became available and more people were able to survive. The new jobs created by manufacturing industries helped the landless proletariat support themselves independently, while some pioneering peasants were able to acquire land and start businesses. New prosperity helped the population to surge, which in turn heightened competition and adversely created a workforce more easily taken advantage of.

In the later stages of the eighteenth century, economists in France and Germany looked for the source of England's economic supremacy in Europe. French economists took Smith's notion of how English wealth came about to explore what lead to the French Revolution and how France might rebuild following it, while German economists were more inspired by Rousseau and his thoughts on the "closed commercial state" that would protect manufacturers and producers while benefitting from commerce.

It is indisputable that commerce transformed Western society in the mid-eighteenth century. Political economy was born of an attempt to understand the science behind the power of commerce and to theorize the most effective way to harness it. For Enlightenment thinkers, the new political economy represented the progress of society and would inevitably lead to human betterment. The shift from an agricultural to a commercial society was so swift that government policies failed to keep up with the cultural and economic change of the Enlightenment era. Despite its limitations and despite the obstacles, the modern commercial economy was so diverse, so powerful, that no government could hope to control it, and that was the most important thing. For many Enlightenment thinkers, the new political economy offered the potential for complete revolution.

Chapter Six

The Enlightenment and the Public

"It is time to effect a revolution in female manners—time to restore to them their lost dignity —and make them, as a part of the human species, labour by reforming themselves to reform the world. It is time to separate unchangeable morals from local manners."

—Mary Wollstonecraft

The great thinkers of the Enlightenment had many ideas about how a person should live, their faith, their morals, how they interacted with society, and how they made their living. The intellectual work of Enlightenment thinkers was expressed, shared, challenged, and re-hashed amongst philosophers and writers for centuries, but the most important ingredient in the Age of Enlightenment, the thing that forced these ideas out of the universities and into the streets, was public opinion.

Some Enlightenment thinkers had a direct impact on the way of life of ordinary people thanks to their relationships with rulers, particularly kings and influential princes. Sometimes leaders invited particular philosophers into their court where those philosophers entertained, educated and, at times, even had an impact on policy-making. A few notorious rulers who engaged with the Enlightenment in this way are Frederick II of Prussia, Joseph II of Austria, and Caroline II of Russia.

But for many of the great thinkers of the Enlightenment, a position at the court of a ruler would be unthinkable. For these men, reaching the ordinary citizens of their nation and playing a role in the formation of public opinion was of the utmost importance. As the authority of the Church, the monarchy, and the government began to wane in the late eighteenth century, a new public sphere emerged. For the first time in Europe, people from many different walks of life were able to socialize together in the city, and it became far less scandalous for people from different social classes to mix.

In England, the emergence of the coffee house was pivotal to this new public sphere. The first coffee houses emerged in England and the trend soon spread into Paris and across Europe until, in the late eighteenth century, establishments where people met to drink coffee became commonplace. Far more refined and sociable than the taverns that preceded them, coffee shops became places to meet for intelligent conversation and enlightening debate. Suddenly people became coffee and chocolate connoisseurs and spent hours in their favorite cafés reading and discussing whatever it is they might have read.

Another institution that linked the Enlightenment with the public sphere was the salon. In the mid-eighteenth century, Paris became the home of many salons and attracted the most notable philosophers and writers of the time. Essentially social gatherings amongst Paris' social and intellectual elites, salons were more often than not organized by women. These women included the wives, friends, and lovers of the leading philosophes of the time, a detail that has led some historians to point to the salons as an example of female agency. The salons, it is thought, offered a space where these women could become involved in the intellectual project of the Enlightenment, inspiring and directing conversation between the men they brought together in their homes.

While this assertion is heartening it is perhaps overly optimistic. The women involved in the Parisian salons of eighteenth-century France were always aristocratic, and their intellectual involvement was limited. A more interesting example of female agency during the Enlightenment can be found in England, where a group of women known as the Bluestockings were recognized for their own intellectual and artistic output, independent of the men they were married to or otherwise involved with. Mary Wollstonecraft is perhaps the most famous female writer to emerge during this time, and her *Vindication of the Rights of Women* (1792) remains one of the key texts of the Enlightenment. In it, Wollstonecraft argues that women are no way inferior to men—they only appear to be due to a lack of education. Wollstonecraft's work represents a feminist approach to basic Enlightenment principles that human beings are rational and should live in a society based on reason, not prejudice.

Chapter Seven

Print Culture and the Press

"The printing press is the greatest weapon in the armory of the modern commander."

—T.E. Lawrence

The printing press, invented in the year 1440, spread across Europe over the course of the next several decades. Even during the earliest days of the Enlightenment, the technology of printing was widespread, and most people were fairly used to seeing the printed word, if only in Bibles, sermons, and other religious works. What changed during the Enlightenment was the scale and sophistication of publishing houses. The volume of books published, and the diversity of what they contained, grew rapidly throughout the eighteenth century until narrative (novels, histories), philosophical, and political books were published in high numbers.

Publishers were businessmen and needed to see a return on their investment once the books they produced went on sale. Certain leading writers enjoyed the success of seeing their work become bestsellers, such as Adam Smith's *Wealth of Nations*, but no Enlightenment text was as popular as D'Alembert and Diderot's *Encyclopédie*. This juggernaut of Enlightenment thought condensed the spirit of the philosophes into an authoritative tome that denounced superstitious religion, overbearing governments, and the power of the monarchy while celebrating human freedom, the new science, and social progress. *Encyclopédie* did not only contain writing by Enlightenment philosophes, it also included critical essays by scientists, tradesmen, and other experts in their fields.

Although expensive to produce (the book was printed in 17 volumes and 11 plates) the financial reward far outweighed the costs. The first publisher of *Encyclopédie* made a huge sum of money before passing the rights on to another publisher whose aggressive business strategies enabled him to distribute the book in France without paying any customs fees. The publisher, named Pancouke, made an astounding amount of money but also benefitted readers by bringing this important book into the homes of up to 16,000 people by the year 1789. The people exposed to *Encyclopédie* ranged from other philosophers, thinkers, and writers of the Enlightenment, aristocrats, and the bourgeoisie as well as the clergy.

It's also worth noting the impact women had on the creation and distribution of the *Encyclopédie*. Many salonnieres, (women associated with the literary and philosophical meet-ups known as salons) contributed to *Encyclopédie* financially and intellectually. Mademoiselle de Lespinasse was a friend of d'Alembert, one of *Encyclopédie*'s editors, and assisted d'Alembert in editing the work as well as using her salon as a forum for discussion of prospective contributions. Other Enlightenment philosophes relied on women to support them in their work: Voltaire was taught science by Madame du Chatelet, the Marquis de Condorcet was intellectually matched by his wife Sophie, who held her own salons, and

Madame de Geoffrin contributed 200,000 livres to the creation of the *Encyclopédie*.

With a new economic incentive to encourage publishing and improve printing technology, the written works of the Enlightenment could reach more people than ever before—and yet two things still stood in the way of truly reaching the public: censorship and illiteracy. The approach to censoring the distribution of the written word varied dramatically in different European countries under different rulers.

In England, there was very little done to regulate publishing once the Licensing Act lapsed in 1695 and intellectual life was rarely impacted by libel laws. In France, by comparison, the Director of Book Trade worked with the police to enforce bans on works they deemed inappropriate. In Prussia, where Frederick II was in power, the approach to book censorship was liberal, while in Germany the attitude changed on a state-by-state basis. Overall, Europe's attempt to control publishing and the distribution of printed matter was inconsistent and failed to curb the growing market for books.

That the market for books was growing at all suggests that literacy was on the rise. In France, historians estimate that literacy grew from around a quarter of the male population to around half between the late seventeenth and late eighteenth century. For women, literacy increased from around 14% of the population to around a quarter during the same time. In England, literacy rose even more dramatically; by the end of the eighteenth century up to 60% of men were literate and 40% of women. These figures paint a heartening picture, but it should be noted that literacy rates were markedly higher in urban centers; in rural parts of these countries, most people were still unable to read.

For those who were fortunate enough to be literate during this time, deciding which books to buy (and having the funds to pay for them) was still an issue. In this newly accessible literary landscape, it was up to authors to shape their own readership. Authorship became an important part of print culture—for the first time the author's name became the focal point of the book cover, and many publishers included a list of the author's credentials and previous works. Authors also experimented with format, realizing that shorter, cheaper books would sell in greater numbers than the leather-bound volumes they had published previously. Authors began to sell the copyright of their works to publishers, buying themselves the independence to work on whatever they chose, instead of being beholden by taking university positions, patronage, or even invitations to court to fund their writing.

Authors were also able to attract new readers and promote their work through innovations in the literary world, such as essay competitions and literary review journals. By encouraging reviews of their latest work or contributing to the review journals themselves, these writers became authoritative voices in the literary world. Essay competitions are commonplace today, but in their initial incarnation, prize essay contests could make or break a writer's reputation. The essay competition offered each year by the Royal Academy of Arts and Sciences in Berlin was one of the most prestigious and influential and jump-started the writing career of two of its most original winners, J. D. Michaels in 1759 and J. G. Herder in 1771.

By the mid to late eighteenth century, Enlightenment thought had gone some way in transforming university education, particularly in the northern parts of Europe. Writers such as John Locke and Jean Jacques Rousseau wrote about educational theory, emphasizing the importance of educating the young and suggesting effective methods for teaching and learning. The progressive principles of the Enlightenment were adopted by a number of universities such as Edinburgh, Göttingen, Halle, and Montpellier but for the most part, educational institutions were founded on traditional principles that were too deeply ingrained to allow room for Enlightenment-inspired reform.

Learning academies, by comparison, recognized the influence of Enlightenment philosophers in intellectual and literary life and welcomed them into their institutions. Initially learning academies in Europe were very closely tied to the state or the monarchy. In France, academies hosted regular academic contests that encouraged entries from all walks of life and supported engagement with controversial subjects such as the role of the monarchy, the scientific theories of Isaac Newton, the slave trade, and women's rights. Thanks to the anonymity of the contestants, a number of women and people from the working class won competitions. In England, the Royal Society of London also worked to spread the ideas of the Enlightenment throughout the public sphere. Founded by a group of independent scientists, the society was a place of experimentation and discussion and helped to legitimize and promote the findings of Enlightenment scientists.

At the heart of all of this—all of the philosophizing and intellectual sparring in coffee houses and salons and academies, and the publishing and distributing of the written word—was the Enlightenment thinkers' desire to shape public opinion. By educating the public on matters previously kept under wraps, such as the economic position of the nation, affairs of state, and royal finances, Enlightenment philosophers encouraged open debate on political policy. Public opinion began to play a pivotal role in politics, and Enlightenment philosophers led the way in informing and empowering public opinion to conform with their ideas on the progress of society.

Conclusion

The legacy of the Enlightenment reaches far enough in time to be relevant today and wide enough in scope to have affected the whole world. The Enlightenment marked the optimistic beginnings of the global village we are now all part of, facilitated by the all-seeing eye and ever-reaching hand of the internet.

Our differences from each other once represented nothing but a threat. Our world today is still divided into nations that seem determined not to get along, but the idea that we should be in harmony, that an ideal society is one in which every human being is equal, is a product of the Enlightenment. To be progressive, to be educated, to be rational, and to be liberal, all of these qualities are considered desirable in a person and became so as a result of the Enlightenment. To be cosmopolitan and to consider yourself a citizen of the world rather than your specific corner of it was encouraged by Enlightenment philosophers who wanted to see the world united under a common way of life informed by reason and rationality alone. Generally speaking, Enlightenment philosophers believed that with only a few civil laws and simple moral codes that are themselves inherent, every member of the human race would be part of a global enlightened nation.

But this revolutionary idea and the movement that it created was not without its victims. Considered from the perspective of a colonized or otherwise persecuted member of the human race who was alive during the time the Enlightenment was still very much a project, it seemed that the whole premise was doomed to fail. For some, the

Enlightenment only encouraged Eurocentrism and fortified the West's belief that it was superior to the rest of the world. During this period in history, the West colonized, oppressed, and exploited the people of other nations and races on a grander scale than ever before. The Age of Enlightenment was also the Age of the Slave Trade.

While for some the Enlightenment was the precursor to the scientific revolution and the glories of modernity, for others it was the precursor to modern imperialism and racism. Where some might point to the Enlightenment's claim that all human beings are equal and need only look to reason to find salvation, others see the Enlightenment's intolerance of everything that challenged its rationalistic and reductive outlook. By attempting, with one great sweep of the arm, to clear the table of the traditions and beliefs of human cultures that have evolved over very long periods of time, the Enlightenment enslaved in conformity the very people they were supposed to set free. Some historians believe that attempts to force this rational, ideal, enlightened worldview on the masses have resulted in human tragedy on an epic scale—such as the French Revolution, the Russian Revolution, and the Chinese Revolution.

Few other movements in history have been the subject of as much study, debate, and writing as the Enlightenment. What the Enlightenment was and why it still matters today preoccupies the intellectual life of many and is a subject this book has tried to illuminate for readers today.

Made in the USA
Monee, IL
12 September 2023